DESIGNED TO LOVE

Designed to Love: Discovering God's Call Through the Four Transcendental Paths

Published by Jonah Company
Purcellville, VA
jonahcompany.com
transcendentaltypes.com

ISBN: 979-8-9948580-0-4 (paperback)

Scripture quotations are from the Revised Standard Version Catholic Edition (RSV-CE), unless otherwise noted.

Printed in the United States of America.

DESIGNED TO LOVE

Discovering God's Call Through the Four Transcendental Paths

BY KRISTY MALIK

CONTENTS

FOREWORD

A CALL TO AWAKEN

By Thomas Cavanaugh

Jonah was called to Nineveh—a city he feared, hated, and wanted nothing to do with. So, he ran. And when the storms came, he asked to be thrown into the sea. But God, in His mercy, didn't let the story end there. He sent a fish, not to punish Jonah, but to preserve him. To make space for transformation.

That story, as strange and ancient as it sounds, is more relevant now than ever. Because God is still calling prophets—often reluctant ones. People like me. People like you. He's still sending us to the places and people we fear, because that's where His mercy wants to go.

In the belly of that fish, Jonah remembered who God is. And in remembering, he began to rediscover who he was. That's the moment we're all waiting for: that sacred clarity when fear dissolves and calling rises. When love becomes stronger than self-protection. When mission feels possible again.

I've had those moments in the least likely places. I left formal ministry a few years ago and stepped into the business world, uncertain of what God was doing. What began as consulting for executives became something more surprising, and far more personal. People began asking me about faith. Quietly. Desperately.

It didn't happen in Bible studies or church groups; it happened in boardrooms, gyms, and late-night conversations. These people were thriving in the world's eyes. But inwardly, they were starving.

I was, too.

In that wilderness, I began to see my own story more clearly—not as a detour from mission, but as *the* mission. God wasn't done with me. He was inviting me deeper. And the story that gave language to it all was Jonah's.

That's what this book is really about: not strategies, not categories, but calling.

A call to remember who God is. And in that remembering, to rediscover who you are.

The framework you'll encounter in these pages is not something we invented. It's something we received. And it's changed lives, not because it's clever, but because it speaks to something God has already placed in you: a sacred way of seeing, loving, and living.

The world is saturated with voices, but starving for vision. It doesn't need more volume. It needs more prophets who know how to love. Prophets willing to go to their Nineveh — not because they have all the answers, but because they've heard the call.

You may not feel ready. You may not feel like a prophet. But if your heart is stirring — even a little — I want you to know: You're not alone. You're not behind. And you are not forgotten. You are being called, and the time has come.

My prayer is that this book stirs that call in you. That you would remember who God is. And in that remembering, rediscover the truth of who you are. That you would learn to love as you were made to love — and through your love, others might encounter the living Christ.

It's time to go to Nineveh.

— Thomas

INTRODUCTION

DESIGNED TO LOVE

You are not here by accident.

If you're reading this, something in your spirit is already stirring—something that knows there is more. More to God than you've yet encountered. More to you than you've fully understood. More to love than you've been taught to expect.

This book begins with that longing, not with a list of answers, but with a deeper question: *How were you made to love?*

Because before love becomes something you *do*, it is something you *receive*. And before you can receive it fully, you must understand how you were made.

What you're about to explore isn't a personality theory. This is a theological map–a way of understanding the soul through the lens of divine design.

At the center is a framework we call the Transcendental Types, or T-Types. Rooted in Scripture, Tradition, and centuries of theological insight, the T-Types reveal something extraordinary: that each of us reflects one primary aspect of God's own nature—Truth, Goodness, Unity, or Beauty—and that this reflection shapes how we encounter Him, how we love others, and how we are called to grow.

These four paths are not arbitrary. They are drawn from the vision of the prophet Ezekiel, echoed by the early Church Fathers, and imprinted on every page of the Gospels. They are not fixed identities, but spiritual starting points; ways of perceiving and returning divine love.

In this book, you'll:

- Discover which path—Truth, Goodness, Unity, or Beauty—is most natural to you.
- Learn how that path reveals both your gifts and your greatest temptations.
- See how each of the four Gospels uniquely reflects one aspect of Christ's nature and how your heart may already be drawn to one of them.
- Explore how your design can shape your relationships, heals wounds, and clarifies your call.

You'll also begin to recognize how love is not just a virtue to practice, but a lens through which you see and are seen. You'll explore how the Spirit and Flesh mindsets - two distinct postures of the soul - influence your behavior and how grace makes true transformation possible.

Above all, you'll be reminded: you were designed to love. Not generically. Not abstractly. But personally, intimately, intentionally, according to the very image of God within you.

This is the gift you've been given. And it's the gift the Church desperately needs you to share.

So let this book be a mirror. Let it show you who you are and Whose you are. Let it remind you of what your heart has always known: that your way of seeing is not accidental, and your way of loving deeply matters.

And as you read, don't be surprised if you find yourself saying yes to something bigger than you imagined.

That yes is the beginning of every great mission. Just ask Jonah.

Let's begin.

CHAPTER 1

THE GREAT COMMANDMENT: LOVE AS THE MISSION, NOT THE ADD-ON

They don't tell you this on your wedding day, but marriage is not just a union. It's a classroom.

Venerable Archbishop Fulton Sheen once said that *"marriage is the school of divine love."* Beautiful, right?

At the beginning of my marriage, I would've focused only on the "divine love" part. I assumed that if you had a good marriage, it would look like heaven: peaceful, harmonious, effortless, maybe even a little perfect.

But after 20 years, I've come to realize that the word I would have initially overlooked was the most important one: *school.*

We're not born knowing how to love like God. We're born with the capacity for love — we love our parents, our pets, our favorite things — but as we grow, that love becomes tangled by fear, pride, insecurity, and sin. What begins as natural affection has to be formed, purified, and directed toward its divine source.

That kind of love — *divine love* — must be taught. And not just in words, but through example. That's why God doesn't just command us to love. He shows us how.

Jesus does this most perfectly. In His mercy, God also sends people into our lives to teach us, to show us, in flesh and blood, how to love and be loved. For me, one of those people has been my husband.

Here's one lesson I've learned in my own "classroom":

At the start of our marriage, I believed what many of us do: that a good relationship is one without conflict. I thought harmony meant ease: if we didn't fight, we must be fine. So when disagreements came (as they always do), I didn't know what to do with them. My instinct was to avoid, dismiss, or rush past the discomfort. Smile, smooth things over, keep moving. I thought: *If we don't fight, we must be fine.*

My husband, steady, present, and deeply loving, had a different instinct. In the Transcendental Type framework, he is *the Peacemaker*, so he didn't let my silence pass for peace. He didn't push or demand, but he stayed. He listened. He invited. He gently drew me into a space I didn't know how to enter yet — one where real love meant staying in the mess long enough to heal it.

It was difficult at first. I wanted to run, not from him, but from the fear of being misunderstood or the shame of being wrong. However, he didn't leave. He didn't accuse. He was just there asking questions, sharing honestly, waiting with hope.

That constancy changed me.

Slowly, I began to see that love isn't the absence of conflict. Love is what you choose when conflict arises. It's the daily decision to lean in when everything in you wants to shut down. It's communion in the tension. Reconciliation in the middle of misunderstanding. Presence that doesn't waver when emotions do.

And it was in those quiet, imperfect, faithful moments that I saw it: my husband's love was just a glimpse. A reflection. A living icon of how God loves us.

God doesn't walk away when we're messy. He doesn't avoid hard conversations or wait for us to clean up before He draws near. He stays. He listens. He loves us, right there in the confusion, the shame, the silence.

That's the kind of love we're *called to*, and that's the kind of love we were *made for*.

That realization opened a door in me.

What if love isn't just *one* commandment among many?
What if love is the whole mission?

Jesus didn't come just to give us new rules or better theology, He came to reveal the Father. The essence of that revelation is this: *God is love.* Not an abstract love, but a love that dwells with us, weeps with us, dies for us, and lives in us. A love that transforms.

In this chapter, we'll explore why the Great Commandment — to love God with all your heart, soul, mind, and strength, and to love your neighbor as yourself — isn't just a spiritual goal. It's the center of the Gospel. It's what every doctrine, sacrament, and spiritual gift is ordered toward.

That's where the Transcendental Types come in. Unlike many ministries that faithfully teach truth and beauty, this framework goes a step further: it shows us how to be *formed* in love, how to receive it, return it, and live it as our deepest mission.

Let's begin there.

In the Catholic Church today, we are surrounded by ministries doing beautiful, vital work. Some teach us the truth through apologetics, catechesis, and moral theology. Others unveil the beauty of the Church's sacramental life through reverent liturgy, breathtaking art, and theological tradition. Some courageously proclaim the goodness of Christ's teachings in the face of cultural pressure — upholding the dignity of life, the gift of sexuality, and the authority of the Church in matters of faith and morals.

These are treasures. We need them, but they are not the end.

They are means.

Every law, sacrament, and doctrine is ordered toward something greater than itself: *the Great Commandment.*

To love God with all our heart, soul, mind, and strength — and to love our neighbor as ourselves. That is the mission. That is the goal. That is the whole.

Yet in all our formation, too many of us have not yet been taught how to love. Not just the command to love, but how to receive love, how to return it, and how to live in it.

This is the missing center.

We know about God, but we don't always know how to be transformed by Him. We can explain the Scripture, defend the sacraments, and share Church teaching, but still feel distant from the One who gave it all.

That's why Jesus came. Not just to reveal information, but to restore communion with God.

To love as Jesus loves - with divine, self-giving love - requires not just correct belief or obedience, but a real *interior participation in the divine life*. This means allowing the life of God – his love, His truth, His Spirit – to dwell within us and transform us from the inside out. According to Christian teaching, this is not optional but essential: through baptism and the sacraments, especially the Eucharist, we are invited into *communion* with God, not just intellectual agreement. As St. Peter writes, we become "partakers of the divine nature" (2 Peter 1:4 RSV) and St. Paul says, "It is no longer I who live, but Christ who lives in me" (Galatians 2:20 RSV).

The early Church Fathers knew this. The mystics lived it. The saints bore witness to it. Salvation is not merely moral conformity or intellectual assent, but union with God. As St. Athanasius wrote, "God became man so that man might become God."

Love is not peripheral. Love is not optional. Love is the core. It is the aim of every prayer, every doctrine, every Mass, every act of penance. Without love, we are nothing.

And yet, love is not generic. It is not one-size-fits-all.

Each of us receives and returns love uniquely according to how we were made in God's image. That's the essence behind the Transcendental Types - or "T-Types" - a framework born not from branding, but from calling. It's also why we chose the name *Jonah*: because like him, we are often reluctant prophets, called to love in places we'd rather avoid - and transformed in the process.

The T-Types are not a personality test. They are not a gimmick. They are a map. A theological, psychological, and spiritual framework for rediscovering how each soul is uniquely designed to encounter God — and to become a living image of Him in the world.

If love is the mission, we must understand how love begins...and it starts with perception.

Before we can learn to love as Christ loves, we must understand how we see Him — because every soul perceives and receives God's love in a unique way. That is why our story must begin with how we were made in His image.

JONAH'S PARALLEL

The Call That Feels Too Big

Jonah's story didn't begin with a yes. His story began with a call — one that interrupted his expectations. "Go to Nineveh," God said, "and proclaim what I tell you." Instead of obedience, He fled. He ran in the opposite direction — not because he lacked capacity, but because the mission felt too big, too unknown. And yet, the call remained. The first movement of every story of love is not our choice — but God's. He comes near. He calls. He asks us to love in ways that challenge our assumptions, just as He did for Jonah. The question is never just, "Are we capable?" It's, "Are we willing?"

CHAPTER 2

MADE IN HIS IMAGE: WHY YOU SEE GOD THE WAY YOU DO

The Question That Started It All

What if the way you see God isn't random?

What if it's not just about personality, upbringing, or experience, but about design?

Before we can love like Christ, we must see Him. And the way each of us first sees Him — whether as Truth, Goodness, Unity, or Beauty — is not incidental. It's theological. It's how we were made. A priest once told me "God is an artist, and he leaves his imprint on everything He creates."

As I came to understand the T-Types, I realized this isn't just a new framework for categorizing people. It's a theology of the person. Each of us bears one of God's attributes more vividly — but we are all called to become whole, to reflect all four in Christ. This journey isn't about staying in one lane; it's about discovering how love begins, and then growing in every direction love can go.

That understanding first stirred in me one night a few years ago...

I first heard my friend Thomas mention the "T-Types" one night a few years ago during an event I attended with my husband, and I'll be honest, part of me was intrigued, and part of me was skeptical. Thomas always spoke with conviction about his beliefs, and this was no different. He mentioned how different "Types" reflect the image of God and how they experience God and other people differently. He said it was like the enneagram, but rooted in Christianity. He's seen it play out with countless people he's encountered through the years. He shared stories of marriages and families and individuals, all who had been transformed by this system called "The Transcendental Types."

It sounded fascinating, even beautiful. Initially, I brushed it off as just an interesting theory. (Personality types were always something that I found interesting, but then felt like they boxed me in. So what if I'm a 1 on the Enneagram or an ESTJ in Meyers Briggs?) The topic of the T-Types surfaced a few more times in our conversations, and I began to wonder if it was true. Where did it come from? Could this really be something that could help me know, love, and serve God better and, in turn, my neighbor? I've always thought that if something truly comes from God, it can stand up to the light of reason. Over the next few months, I decided to investigate the T-Types further.

What opened the door for me wasn't just curiosity, it was an encounter.

I've always believed that God is true, that His Word is trustworthy, and that what Scripture teaches is reality, even when I couldn't feel it. My faith was anchored in that conviction: truth doesn't depend on my emotions. I leaned on that certainty through years of dryness and unanswered questions.

However, God didn't just want my assent, He wanted my whole heart.

During a time of prayer at a retreat, the Holy Spirit brought to mind a wound I had carried for years. It wasn't the first time. He had gently invited me to give it to Him before. But that day, I finally said yes. I handed Him the pain I had kept hidden, the one I thought I had dealt with by simply ignoring.

What happened next changed me.

I was overwhelmed by a sense of warmth and peace — not just emotionally, but physically. My whole body felt flooded with light. I knew, in that moment, that I was being healed. Not symbolically, but physically, emotionally, and spiritually healed.

It was as though everything I had ever believed in my mind about God's love, His power, His nearness finally reached the deepest parts of me. It wasn't just true anymore. It was real. And, like a gentleman, God waited for me to invite Him into my heart.

That experience didn't undo my love for truth, it fulfilled it. God didn't bypass my mind to reach my heart. He used everything I had believed as a pathway to reach all of me.

That was the beginning of a new chapter in my relationship with Him, and a new openness to see how He had made me to receive and return His love in a very specific, personal way. That's where the T-Types began to make sense. Not as a theory, but as a mirror — one that helped me see not only who I am, but how God had always been reaching for me.

The Image of God: The Starting Point

At some point, we all find ourselves asking deeper questions:. *Why do I keep repeating the same patterns? Why does lasting change feel so hard?* Beneath these struggles lies an even deeper longing: to understand *who we are* and *why we're here. What does it mean to be made in the image of God?* The truth is, we are not problems to be solved — we are images of God to be revealed.

Scripture doesn't leave that vague. From the opening pages of Genesis to the face of Christ in the Gospels, God reveals not only who He is, but who we are. To be made in His image means our very way of thinking, feeling, loving, and creating reflects something divine.

In Colossians 1:15, St. Paul writes, "He is the image of the invisible God, the firstborn of all creation." Christ is not just the Son of God — He is the visible face of the invisible God. In Him, we see what God looks like. In Him, we see who we are meant to become.

According to the *Catechism of the Catholic Church* (221), "God's very being is love. By sending His only Son and the Spirit of Love in the fullness of time, God has revealed His innermost secret: God Himself is an eternal exchange of love, Father, Son, and Holy Spirit, and he has destined us to share in that exchange."

This is where our journey must begin. If we are made in God's image, and Christ is that image made visible, then knowing Him is the key to knowing ourselves. The more clearly we see Him, the more clearly we understand the truth of our own design.

That vision becomes even more striking when we turn to the prophets — especially the vision given to Ezekiel.

The Clues in the Vision of Ezekiel

The first time I reread *Ezekiel 1* with fresh eyes, it felt like a veil had been pulled back. The scene is unlike anything else in Scripture: the heavens open, and the prophet sees "visions of God." A stormy wind, flashes of lightning, and a great fiery cloud appear — and from the midst of it emerge four living creatures. Each one has four faces: a man, a lion, an ox, and an eagle. Their movement is swift and unified, their appearance radiant and terrifying.

THE MAN

THE LION

THE OX

THE EAGLE

It is a mysterious and majestic vision — but not an arbitrary one. For centuries, the Church Fathers have recognized that these four faces represent more than poetic symbolism. They are a revelation. A mirror. A divine blueprint pointing to the way God designed humanity to reflect His own nature: His *Truth*, *Goodness*, *Unity*, and *Beauty*.

These same creatures appear again in *Revelation 4*, this time encircling the throne of the Lamb. St. John describes them in strikingly similar language: "full of eyes in front and behind," constantly crying out, "Holy, holy, holy is the Lord God almighty." Once again, the man, lion, ox, and eagle are not just strange imagery. They are heaven's own icons — revealing something essential about both *who God is* and *who we are made to become*.

This symbolic quartet is often called the *tetramorph* (from the Greek for "four forms"). And it has deeply shaped the Church's theology and imagination.

Jerome's Tetramorph

In his Prologue to the Gospel of Matthew, St. Jerome linked each of the four evangelists to one of these living creatures. Matthew — who begins with Christ's genealogy — is symbolized by the *man*. Mark — who emphasizes the royal power and urgency of Jesus — is the *lion*. Luke — who highlights sacrifice, the poor, and the Incarnation — is the *ox*. And John — whose Gospel soars into the eternal Word made flesh — is the *eagle*.

This interpretation became so foundational that it shaped centuries of Christian iconography. From the Book of Kells to basilica mosaics and Gothic cathedrals, artists depicted Christ enthroned and surrounded by these four living faces. Worshippers saw — and still see — in those symbols a cosmic proclamation: Christ, the fullness of divinity, reveals and restores the fullness of humanity.

St. Irenaeus and the Fourfold Face of Christ

St. Irenaeus of Lyons — bishop, theologian, and martyr of the second century — was among the first to see that Ezekiel's vision was not just prophetic, but profoundly Christological.

In *Against Heresies* (Book III, Chapter 11), he writes:

> "It is not possible that the Gospels can be either more or fewer in number than they are. For... the cherubim are four-faced, and their faces are images of the activity of the Son of God. For the first living creature was like a lion... the second like a calf... the third had the face of a man... the fourth was like a flying eagle."

For Irenaeus, these four living creatures were not random symbols, but visible signs of the one Christ, revealed in four distinct ways:

- **Matthew** as the *man* — Christ the Incarnate Son and Teacher (*Truth*),
- **Mark** as the *lion* — Christ the Powerful King in action (*Goodness*),
- **Luke** as the *ox* — Christ the Priest and Sacrificial Reconciler (*Unity*),
- **John** as the *eagle* — Christ the Eternal Word, soaring into mystery (*Beauty*).

This was not a poetic flourish, but theological precision. In the mystery of the Gospels, the Church beholds not four Jesuses, but one Lord with four radiant faces — each offering a unique window into the divine life.

This same fourfold vision of Christ invites a personal reflection: if Jesus can be revealed through four faces, could it be that each of us is drawn more deeply to one — not to the exclusion of the others, but as a primary path of love?

Could the face we most clearly see... be the one we are uniquely made to reflect?

The Transcendentals: God's Radiance in the Human Person

From this theological vision, we turn to a philosophical one — not as a departure, but as a deepening.

Long before modern psychology, ancient philosophers and Church Fathers asked a deeper question: *How does everything in creation reflect the nature of God?*

The answer lies in what came to be known as the *Transcendentals* — four qualities that are not merely *about* God, but are *of* God Himself: **Truth, Goodness, Unity, and Beauty**.

Plato intuited them. St. Augustine pondered them. St. Thomas Aquinas refined them with remarkable clarity. For Aquinas, these are not categories, but the very qualities that mark God's being — and by extension, ours.

They are not personality types. They are divine fingerprints.

- **Truth** reveals the clarity and order of God's mind.
- **Goodness** expresses His will to love and redeem.
- **Unity** reflects the communion of the Trinity, the oneness that binds all things in love.
- **Beauty** unveils the radiance and harmony of His presence.

We each naturally resonate more deeply with one of these — not by accident, but by design. It's the path through which we most easily perceive God's love, and the way we most instinctively return it.

And that is why, in the Transcendental Type framework, we speak of these not simply as theological abstractions, but as living vocations.

Each of us bears one of these transcendentals in a primary way — not to limit us, but to illuminate the path by which we love and are loved.

A Note on Language:
In classical philosophy, the transcendental often listed as "the One" (unum) is most faithfully translated as *Unity* (unitas). St. Thomas describes it not as simple singularity, but as the power of harmony — the energy of communion. We use "Unity" to capture this dynamic quality — not a departure from tradition, but its fullest expression.

The Gospels: Four Portraits, One Lord

When I saw how perfectly each Gospel aligns with one of the Transcendentals, it stopped me. It wasn't just intellectually satisfying — it was spiritually illuminating.

- Matthew reveals the mind of Christ — the Truth that fulfills every law.
- Mark shows the courage and action of divine Goodness.
- Luke opens the heart of Unity that reconciles all things.
- John lifts us into the mystery of divine Beauty that makes heaven touch earth.

This isn't psychology. This is divine revelation. The fingerprints of the Creator are on every page of Scripture — and every human soul.

The T-Types flow from this: four ways of seeing, four ways of loving, all drawing us toward the One Lord who is the fullness of Truth, Goodness, Unity, and Beauty.

Art and the Tetramorph

Christian communities didn't just read these truths — they lived them. In mosaics, illuminated texts, and basilica domes, the four creatures surrounded Christ in worship. They weren't decorations — they were declarations. Declarations that Christ is the fullness of God's image, and we are made to reflect that image in all its facets.

Pictured: Fresco (16th Century); Ivory and Wood Carving (13th Century); Book of Kells (9th century)

Why It Matters

The more I studied, the more I realized: this isn't just a new way of categorizing people. It's a theology of the person. We each reflect one aspect of God more vividly, but we are all called to become whole — to reflect all four in Christ.

Knowing our "transcendental lens" isn't about labeling ourselves; it's about learning how to love more like Him. It gives us a starting point — a spiritual compass — not to limit our growth but to expand it. When we know how we most naturally encounter God, we can be more intentional in how we grow toward Him and how we love those who see Him differently.

Just as the four Gospels present one Christ in four lights, our souls each begin with a dominant lens through which we see God most clearly, and often most instinctively. This doesn't mean the others are closed off to us. On the contrary, spiritual maturity involves growing into all four — truth, goodness, unity, and beauty — until, as St. Paul instructs in Ephesians 4:15, "we should grow in every way into him who is the head, Christ."

The Truth That Satisfied My Mind and Moved My Heart

For someone like me, who's wired for Truth, the T-Types had to pass the test of coherence — they needed to be biblically grounded, theologically sound, and philosophically consistent. To my surprise, they were. The more I searched, the more I found that this framework wasn't a modern invention, but an ancient mirror of the Gospel itself.

In discovering that truth, I didn't just understand myself better, I met Christ more personally than ever before.

The more I explored, the more I realized this wasn't just a new lens for personality; it was a window into the mystery of God Himself. The Transcendentals aren't theories; they're traces of His face imprinted on every human soul. When I finally stopped analyzing long enough to pray with it, something unexpected happened — I recognized myself. I came to realize that the longing I experienced in needing to make sense of the world and of God wasn't pride or stubbornness; it was His own mind alive in me, seeking its source.

That's when it clicked: we each reflect one of these divine pathways — Truth, Goodness, Unity, or Beauty — not as a limit, but as an invitation. You were made to see God in a certain way because He intends to meet you there.

The question isn't just who am I, but how has God made Himself visible through me?

That's where we'll go next: into the four great ways of seeing and loving Him, to discover which one is the starting place for your story with God, and how that vision shapes every act of love that follows.

JONAH'S PARALLEL

Remembering Who God is in the Dark

In the depths—literally in the belly of the fish—Jonah cried out: 'Out of my distress I called to the Lord, and he answered me.' (Jonah 2:3) He remembered who God is. In that remembering, his own identity began to surface. That turning inward led him outward again. When we wrestle with our identity — Who am I? — that image of God in us is never lost. Even in our exile or failure, God meets us in the depths and calls us back to who we truly are.

CHAPTER 3

FOUR WAYS WE LOVE: DISCOVERING YOUR TRANSCENDENTAL TYPE

Each of us sees God a little differently. Not because He changes, but because He meets us where we are. Like the four evangelists who told the one Gospel from four angles, each of us reflects a unique facet of His glory — Truth, Goodness, Unity, or Beauty.

These aren't just ideas. They are ways of loving.

They're the paths through which we encounter God. and the paths through which we are called to love others.

Let's explore each one through the life of a saint: someone who shows us what love looks like when it's fully alive in a particular way. You'll also find a simple reflection with each section to help you begin discerning your own T-Type.

The Truth Type: Clarity and Conviction

Saint Thomas Aquinas and St. Edith Stein

Truth types are drawn to clarity, order, and the beauty of reality as it actually is. They tend to be seekers of understanding, often naturally attracted to Scripture, theology, philosophy, or Church teaching. They love studying the Catechism, reading encyclicals, or leading Bible studies — not to win arguments, but to make Christ known.

St. Thomas Aquinas spent his life seeking clarity, not just for himself, but for the whole Church. His philosophical mind wasn't dry or detached; it burned with a desire to know and proclaim the Truth who is Christ. His writings, especially the *Summa Theologiae*, are not just theological blueprints, but acts of worship. When Christ appeared to him near the end of his life and asked, "What do you desire?" Thomas answered, "Nothing but You, Lord."

St. Teresa Benedicta of the Cross (Edith Stein) was a brilliant philosopher who was raised in a Jewish family and later becoming an atheist. Her relentless search for truth led her to read the life of St. Teresa of Ávila, which pierced her heart. She converted to Catholicism and eventually became a Carmelite nun. Her writings on empathy and personhood are as intellectually rigorous as they are spiritually rich. She died in Auschwitz, offering her life in union with Christ.

Truth Types are seekers. They ask, investigate, clarify, and commit. They aren't content with vague feelings or surface answers. They want to understand. Once they find the truth, they stand by it, even when it costs them everything.

Yet they also face a particular cross: the temptation to idolize certainty, to detach from emotion, or to become critical of those who don't "get it" as quickly. Grace calls them to integrate head and heart: to let truth serve love.

Reflection: What questions have led you closer to God? Do you feel most alive when learning or explaining truth?

The Goodness Type: Compassion and Justice

St. Elizabeth Ann Seton and St. Ignatius of Loyola

Goodness Types are doers. They are drawn to the needs of others, especially those who are suffering, overlooked, or unjustly treated. They experience God most clearly in acts of mercy, concrete service, and social mission. Many find their vocations in education, healthcare, community leadership, or advocacy. Their lives are rooted in the corporal and spiritual works of mercy.

St. Elizabeth Ann Seton, the first American-born saint, was a wife, mother, widow, convert, and foundress. After losing her husband and facing deep personal grief, she turned her pain into compassion and action. She opened schools and orphanages, founded the Sisters of Charity, and helped lay the foundation of Catholic education in America. Her life was marked by tireless service and a profound trust in God's providence.

St. Ignatius of Loyola, the founder of the Jesuits, was once a soldier obsessed with honor and ambition. After a cannonball shattered his leg, he underwent a deep spiritual conversion. From his convalescence came the *Spiritual Exercises*, a tool that has helped countless souls discern God's will. Ignatius poured himself into mission educating the young, confronting injustice, and sending his companions to the far corners of the world, always with the motto: *Ad Majorem Dei Gloriam*, for the greater glory of God.

Goodness Types want to fix what's broken. Their love is practical, grounded, and sacrificial. Their strength is action. Their cross is often burnout: carrying burdens that aren't theirs to carry, or confusing love with control. Grace calls them to surrender; to do what they can, and entrust the rest to God.

Reflection: Do you often feel compelled to help others? Do you find God most clearly in acts of mercy or service?

The Unity Type: Wholeness and Reconciliation

St. Francis of Assisi and St. Kateri Tekakwitha

Unity Types long for communion. They feel the weight of division in relationships, communities, and within the human heart. They are natural peacemakers, often quiet but deeply attuned to the emotional and spiritual needs of others. They tend to be relational, empathetic, and gifted in hospitality or spiritual friendship.

St. Francis of Assisi began as a wealthy young man chasing glory and comfort until Christ spoke to him from the cross: "Rebuild my Church." From that moment, Francis embraced radical poverty and peace. He reconciled enemies, healed wounds, and preached to both people and animals. His joy was infectious, his humility profound. He brought wholeness where there had been a fracture.

St. Kateri Tekakwitha, the "Lily of the Mohawks," was orphaned young, scarred by smallpox, and later rejected by her own people for her conversion. She bore suffering with gentleness and peace and cultivated her faith steadily through prayer, sacrifice, and small acts of love. She formed little communities of prayer among those who followed her example. Her witness was not loud or fiery, but enduring: her hidden unity with Christ quietly nurtured the soil of hearts, where God could bring forth fruit.

Unity Types listen well, feel deeply, and bring people together. Their presence itself brings peace. Their cross is often absorbing others' emotions or avoiding necessary conflict. Grace gives them the strength to remain present without being consumed: to carry others to Christ, not on their shoulders, but in their prayers.

Reflection: Do you long for connection and peace? Do others come to you for comfort or perspective? Are you able to cast a vision of how things could be?

The Beauty Type: Harmony and Inspiration

St. John of the Cross and St. Hildegard of Bingen

Beauty Types feel deeply. They are often highly sensitive, creative, and attuned to symbols and mystery. They experience God in silence, music, poetry, and worship: places where beauty and suffering intertwine. They may feel at home in Eucharistic adoration, sacred music, or quiet reflection. Many are writers, artists, teachers, or storytellers who see what others miss.

St. John of the Cross, a Carmelite mystic and reformer, was imprisoned for his efforts to renew the order. In the dark silence of his cell, he composed some of the most beautiful spiritual poetry in Church history. His *Spiritual Canticle* and *Dark Night of the Soul* reveal not only the soul's longing for God, but the soul's transformation through suffering into union. His words carry both pain and beauty, pointing to the divine presence in all things.

St. Hildegard of Bingen was a visionary Benedictine abbess, composer, writer, and healer. Her mystical visions were filled with color, light, and cosmic imagery. She saw the harmony of creation as a reflection of the Creator and composed music and texts that expressed the soul's yearning for divine beauty. In a time when women's voices were often silenced, her creativity proclaimed God's glory across art, science, and theology.

Beauty Types express what others feel but cannot name. They long for meaning beneath the surface. Their cross is often the pain of feeling misunderstood or dismissed as "too sensitive." They may be tempted to escape into imagination or despair when life feels too ugly. Grace grounds them in reality and helps them offer beauty to others as a healing balm.

Reflection: When have you felt God in beauty? Are you often moved by music, art, or the deeper meaning of things?

Living Out Your Type

We have a joke in my family that, as a Truth Type, I see things like "a rock." This stems from a scene in a movie we watched when our kids were younger: *A Bug's Life*.

In one scene, Flik (the inventive, dreamer ant — a clear Beauty Type) tries to encourage Dot (a practical, skeptical young royal ant — definitely a Truth Type) by using a metaphor. He picks up a rock and tells her to pretend it's a seed. "Everything that made that giant tree is already contained inside this tiny little seed," he explains. "You just have to give yourself some time. You're still a seed."

Dot immediately corrects him: "But it's a rock."

Flik, exasperated, blurts, "I *know* it's a rock! Don't you think I know a rock when I see a rock!?"

It's a perfect depiction of the dynamic between a Beauty Type who speaks in symbols, possibilities, and future potential and a Truth Type who wants clarity, precision, and facts.

This isn't to say Truth Types lack imagination - far from it - but their starting point will always be grounded in reality.

Each of these four ways of loving is a window into the heart of God. You are not one of these by accident. You were designed this way to receive and reflect divine love in a particular way.

The goal is not to stay in one category forever. The goal is growth. To begin where you are strongest, and from there, become whole.

Here's how each type might look in everyday life:

- **Truth Types** live the Gospel through clarity and integrity. They love sharing wisdom, teaching the faith, and helping others see God's plan. In ministry, they may serve as catechists, writers, or spiritual directors.
- **Goodness Types** bring God's mercy into the world through action. They organize meals, care for the sick, start nonprofits, and rush in when others are hurting.
- **Unity Types** build communion. They are the quiet presence who notices who's missing, makes room for others, and prays in the background while others speak.

- **Beauty Types** reflect the glory of God through creativity and reverence. They are often found in sacred music, liturgy, or spiritual art creating spaces where others encounter the divine.

The T-Types app and upcoming tools will help you dive deeper. For now, take time to reflect on where you feel most at home. Where do you encounter God most clearly? That's where your journey of love begins.

The best place to begin that journey is where the Church has always turned to see the face of Christ most clearly: the Gospels.

JONAH'S PARALLEL

Obedience Without Full Transformation

Jonah eventually obeys God's call and goes to Nineveh, and his message sparks a city-wide repentance. Yet even in his obedience, his heart is unsettled. He did the task, but his spirit was not yet transformed. This tension reminds us: action alone isn't the goal; transformation is. Transformation requires not just obedience, but letting love shape how we see others and ourselves.

CHAPTER 4

THE MIRROR OF CHRIST: FINDING YOUR TRUE SELF IN THE GOSPELS

Each Gospel tells the same story — but not in the same way.

The early Church didn't merge them into one narrative because each evangelist reveals a different facet of Christ, a distinct voice inspired by the Holy Spirit. The diversity isn't a flaw – it's a gift. A mirror held up to the One who cannot be contained by any single perspective.

In that mirror, we find not only Him, but ourselves.

The Gospel of Matthew reveals Jesus as the Teacher: the fulfillment of the Law and the prophets. He speaks with authority, bringing divine clarity to the human condition. This is the Gospel of Truth written to a Jewish audience longing for the Messiah. If you resonate with the Truth Type, Matthew may feel like home. You see Christ in His wisdom, His clarity, His call to intellectual and moral coherence.

We see this especially in the Sermon on the Mount (Matthew 5–7), where Jesus proclaims, "Do not think that I have come to abolish the law or the prophets. I have come not to abolish but to fulfill" (Mt 5:17). He teaches with breathtaking clarity, illuminating the heart of the commandments and calling

His disciples to integrity of thought and action. He embodies Truth not merely as doctrine, but as a path to life.

The Gospel of Mark shows Jesus as the Servant: immediately acting, healing, confronting evil, and moving with power. It's short, fast-paced, and vivid. This is the Gospel of Goodness written for Roman Christians who needed strength and courage under persecution. Goodness Types find Christ here in His bold compassion, His tireless justice, His willingness to suffer for love.

One striking moment of Christ's goodness is found in Mark 1:40–42, where a leper kneels before Him, saying, "If you wish, you can make me clean." Moved with pity, Jesus stretches out His hand, touches him, and says, "I do will it. Be made clean." In that touch, socially forbidden and radically merciful, we see the heart of the Goodness Type: action rooted in love, justice expressed through healing.

The Gospel of Luke reveals Jesus as the great Reconciler: the One who restores what is divided and brings wholeness where there is fracture. This is the Gospel of Unity, written for Gentile believers and emphasizing Christ's universal mission to all people. It is full of stories of healing, forgiveness, and inclusion. Luke's Gospel shows how Jesus unites rich and poor, men and women, Jew and Gentile, all within the Kingdom of God.

One powerful moment comes in the story of Zacchaeus (Luke 19:1–10). A tax collector, despised and isolated, climbs a tree just to glimpse Jesus. Christ stops, calls him by name, and chooses to stay at his house. That single act restores Zacchaeus to his community and to himself. Jesus declares, "Today salvation has come to this house," because unity, both with God and neighbor, is the fruit of true love.

The Gospel of John lifts us into the mystery and majesty of divine love. This is the Gospel of Beauty: intimate, poetic, and contemplative. Written to draw believers into deeper communion, it reveals Jesus as the eternal Word, the radiant Bridegroom, and the source of divine glory. In John, Beauty Types see the soul's longing fulfilled in the presence of God.

One of the most beautiful encounters in John's Gospel is between Jesus and Mary Magdalene at the tomb (John 20:11–18). She is weeping, thinking the body of her Lord has been taken. When He speaks her name — "Mary" — she recognizes Him. It is not a theological argument that opens her eyes, it is beauty made personal. This moment captures the essence of Beauty: the intimacy, the tenderness, the encounter that awakens the heart.

Each Gospel reflects a different dimension of Christ because each was written through a particular lens, for a particular audience, by a particular heart. Each Gospel offers a mirror — one that helps you see not only the face of Christ, but the image of God within yourself.

When you begin to read Scripture through your T-Type, something changes. The Gospels become personal. You begin to hear His voice calling you in the way your heart is most able to receive it.

I'll never forget the moment that John 15:9-11 (*"As the Father loves me, so I also love you. Remain in my love"*) landed in a way it never had before. As a Truth Type, I had always read that passage with an emphasis on the statement itself: *"Jesus loves us like God loves Him."* To me, it was an anchoring reminder of Jesus' divinity — a theological truth I could cling to, and a call to stay close to Him. And it is.

This time, the Holy Spirit gently shifted my gaze.

I had been in a season where I was trying hard to do everything right — in prayer, in parenting, and in ministry. I was tired. I came to this verse in my daily reading, not looking for comfort, but just wanting to stay faithful.

As I read, that one line stopped me: *"Remain in my love."*

Not just my teaching. Not just my will. My love.

It was like a doorway opened. Truth led me in, but beauty met me there. I suddenly imagined what it would mean to actually remain there: to live not just for God, but with Him, in Him, in the place of love. To dwell in joy, to be at home in communion. It wasn't an abstract ideal; it felt real, personal. I felt seen.

Jesus wasn't just asking for me to believe Him. He was inviting me into joy.

I realized that truth isn't meant to fence us in; it's meant to lead us deeper into communion. Into the beauty of being loved.

This is not just about understanding the Bible more deeply. It's about encountering Christ — and through Him, discovering your true self.

The Gospels not only reveal Christ — they reveal us. As you begin to see which "face" of Jesus your heart responds to most, you may also begin to sense the deeper design behind that recognition. You're not simply drawn to a story. You're being invited into a relationship — one uniquely shaped by how God made you to love.

But as you reflect on these patterns — these ways of seeing and loving — a natural question might arise: Is this just another personality framework?

It's a fair question. In a world full of tests, types, and labels, it's easy to assume the T-Types are just another spiritual Enneagram or Catholic Myers-Briggs.

That's why, before we go any further, we need to pause and ask: what makes this different?

JONAH'S PARALLEL

The Missing Mirror

Jonah didn't have the Gospels. He didn't yet know the face of Christ – the full image of divine mercy, justice, and love made visible. If he had, perhaps he would have seen more clearly that God's justice and God's compassion are never in conflict, that every warning is also an invitation, and that transformation is always possible. In Jesus, we see what Jonah struggled to imagine: a God who comes close, who weeps, who heals, who saves. That is the mirror that changes us.

CHAPTER 5

BEYOND PERSONALITY: WHY YOUR TRANSCENDENTAL TYPE IS MORE THAN A TYPE

It's tempting to compare the T-Types to other personality frameworks. After all, there are some surface similarities. Like the Enneagram or the MBTI, the T-Types give language to your instincts, patterns, and preferences. They can help you understand yourself better, recognize your strengths, and work on your weaknesses.

The T-Types were never meant to fit in the same category. This isn't just a system for self-discovery, it's a pathway to transformation.

At its heart, the T-Types are not about personality. They're about love.

Unlike most typologies, which sort us based on temperament or behavior, the T-Types are based on theology: specifically, the ancient insight that we are made in the image of a God who is Truth, Goodness, Unity, and Beauty. These aren't arbitrary categories. They are attributes of God: the qualities by which all creation participates in Him.

That means your T-Type isn't just a psychological trait. It's a **spiritual lens**— a unique way you've been created to receive and reflect divine love.

Where other systems stop at self-awareness, the T-Types point toward holiness. They are not self-contained; they're Christ-oriented. Each one is a starting place, not a box. The goal isn't to stay in your type—it's to grow in grace until you become fully conformed to Christ, who embodies all four.

This is the journey of transformation: as you mature in faith, you begin to see how the Spirit invites you to grow beyond your dominant type and into the others, not by changing who you are, but by expanding your capacity to love based on how you were made.

A Truth Type, drawn to clarity and conviction, is invited into Beauty: to receive wonder, to dwell in mystery. A Beauty Type is drawn into Unity: to reconcile and bring harmony where there is division. A Unity Type is called into Goodness: to take action, to serve, to sacrifice. A Goodness Type, formed by service, is drawn toward Truth: refined and purified by experience.

This isn't linear. It's a spiral of grace. You remain who God made you to be, but as the Spirit transforms your heart, you begin to live more fully into the fullness of love.

This movement is part of what we call the Spirit and Flesh mindsets™. Every T-Type can be lived in one of two ways: in the spirit or in the flesh.

The Spirit mindset is what we're meant for—it's our type aligned with grace, rooted in God's love, and open to transformation. It brings life, communion, and freedom.

A Truth Type in the Spirit speaks with wisdom, listens with humility, and leads with love.

A Goodness Type in the Spirit serves with strength, restores what is broken, and uplifts others with peace.

A Unity Type in the Spirit connects with compassion, fosters harmony, and empowers others to flourish.

A Beauty Type in the Spirit creates with reverence, reveals hidden meaning, and draws others into wonder.

Spirit Mindset

The same type, lived in the Flesh, can become distorted.

The Flesh mindset is what happens when fear, pride, shame, or woundedness take over. It's our type turned inward, protecting the ego instead of pouring out in love.

A Truth Type in the Flesh hides behind knowledge, clings to being right, and may become rigid or arrogant.

A Goodness Type in the Flesh seeks control through service, resents the burdens they carry, and struggles to rest.

A Unity Type in the Flesh avoids conflict at all costs, absorbs others' pain as if it were their own, and may surrender their identity in a misguided attempt to keep the peace.

A Beauty Type in the Flesh becomes absorbed in emotion, idealizes suffering, and detaches from reality.

Flesh Mindset

"It is only through shadows that one comes to know the light." St. Catherine of Siena

This language of Spirit and Flesh comes straight from Scripture. Saint Paul uses this contrast throughout his letters, especially in Romans, to describe the interior battle of every believer:

> "For those who live according to the flesh are concerned with the things of the flesh, but those who live according to the spirit with the things of the spirit. The concern of the flesh is death, but the concern of the spirit is life and peace" (Romans 8:5–6).

Paul isn't just contrasting sin versus virtue. He's describing two ways of being: one dominated by fear and self-preservation, the other opened to God's transforming love. "You are not in the flesh," he writes, "you are in the spirit, if only the Spirit of God dwells in you" (Romans 8:9).

This is the essence of the T-Types journey. Not managing your traits, but surrendering your lens to the Spirit so it can be made fruitful in love.

One of the clearest examples of my flesh mindset as a Truth Type happened many Sundays when our kids were younger (and if I'm being honest, still does occasionally now): trying to get our whole family to Mass on time.

With five kids, it's not just about shoes and hair and getting in the car — it's managing emotions, lost items, spilled juice, and last-minute resistance from someone who suddenly decides they *hate* church clothes. I know this. I expect it. And still, something in me snaps when we're running behind.

Instead of pausing to breathe, or laugh, or even pray, I shift into hyper-efficiency mode. I start barking instructions, tightening my tone, and moving like a drill sergeant through the house. In those moments, I convince myself that we *have* to be on time, because it's church. Because it's right. Because God deserves our best.

I've come to realize that my obsession with punctuality isn't always about reverence. Sometimes, it's about control. It's about protecting my image as someone who gets it right, who follows the rules, and who "knows the truth." In trying so hard to honor the truth of Mass, I sometimes miss the heart of it: grace.

I've had mornings where we've arrived "on time," but with everyone silent, tense, and wounded from the whirlwind we just lived through. I've had other days where we were five minutes late, but entered the church with peace and unity, and two of the kids were in sweatpants and hoodies.

God is still there. His grace is still real. He'd rather receive my honest heart than my perfectly timed arrival.

Spirit and Flesh are not fixed categories — they're dynamics. We move between them daily, even hourly. The key is not perfection, but awareness: learning to recognize when your type is moving in the Spirit and when it's slipping into the Flesh.

That's why grace is always the answer. You don't fix the Flesh by trying harder. You return to grace — through prayer, sacrament, community, and the gentle presence of the Holy Spirit.

The goal is not to be "more of your type" or to use your type as an excuse for why you are the way you are. The goal is to become more like Jesus who is the perfection of all four types. Christ is Truth incarnate, Goodness in action, Beauty made visible, and Unity embodied. He is our model, and the T-Types are simply a map that helps us walk toward Him more intentionally.

Of course, there are limits to every system. Any type can become an excuse. Any framework can become a box. The moment we use it to justify sin, pride, or detachment, we've missed the point. The goal of knowing your type isn't to stay comfortable. It's to grow.

This is why the T-Types don't just describe who you are, they invite you into who you're becoming.

When you know your dominant lens, you can:

- Recognize how you most naturally connect with God
- Understand why others love differently than you do
- Grow in empathy and compassion for the people closest to you
- Name the spiritual challenges you face and the graces God offers you to overcome them
- Begin walking a path toward wholeness in Christ

It's not a shortcut. It's not a trend. It's a framework — one that can awaken your heart and lead you to the way you were made to love.

At the end of the day, this isn't about types.

It's about transformation.

Transformation doesn't happen in isolation; it happens in community. "*For as in one body we have many parts, and all the parts do not have the same function, so we, though many, are one body in Christ and individually parts of one another*" (Romans 12:4–5).

That's where we'll go next — to discover why your particular way of loving matters not only for your personal holiness, but for the life and mission of the Church.

The world doesn't just need more programs. It needs more people who love like Christ.

It needs you.

JONAH'S PARALLEL

Resisting the Stretch of Grace

Jonah's final chapter is especially uncomfortable, albeit poignant. He is angry that God spares Nineveh. Jonah had fulfilled his role, but grace still offended him. "I knew that you are a gracious and merciful God... slow to anger, abounding in love..." (Jonah 4:2) His problem wasn't theological. It was relational. He didn't want God to be that merciful. This is the tension we all face: when God stretches our hearts beyond what feels fair, familiar, or safe. Growth isn't about perfecting our type — it's about letting the Spirit expand us beyond it.

CHAPTER 6

YOU ARE NEEDED: WHY THE CHURCH TREASURES YOUR GIFT

If you've ever wondered whether your way of loving God and others is "enough," this chapter is for you.

The truth is: your gift is not only valid — it's essential.

The Church isn't complete without your presence. Your lens. Your way of seeing and reflecting divine love. You were made in the image of God, and that image was never meant to remain hidden. It's meant to shine through you for the good of others.

We've seen it happen over and over again in our work with parishes, schools, ministries, and families. When a team or family learns how to recognize each other's T-Types, everything shifts. There's more compassion in conflict. More clarity in decisions. More creativity in problem-solving. More joy in mission.

In one parish, we saw a leadership team transform when they realized their tension wasn't personal — it was transcendental. The Truth Types wanted clarity and theological precision. The Beauty Types longed for inspiration and design. The Goodness Types focused on justice and serving the poor. The Unity Types fought for harmony and inclusivity. They weren't enemies, they were different parts of the same body, each playing a role.

When they learned to honor each other's instincts, their ministry deepened. The Truth Types helped everyone stay grounded in doctrine. The Beauty Types elevated the experience of worship. The Goodness Types led the charge in community outreach. The Unity Types wove it all together.

This is what the Church looks like when we stop competing and start collaborating. When we stop comparing and start calling out the gifts in each other.

God has given *you* a gift the Church desperately needs.

If you're a **Truth Type**, we need your clarity: your hunger for what is real, what is right, what is eternal. You often carry the torch of conviction when others are tempted to compromise. You remind us who God is when we forget. Don't forget to let Beauty soften you to see wonder, not just rules, to delight in mystery, not just defend the message. Your mind is strong, but let your heart be open too.

Ask yourself:

- When has truth brought me closer to love?
- Do I allow myself to wonder, or do I always need to be right?
- How might Jesus be inviting me to dwell in beauty without fear?

If you're a **Goodness Type**, we need your heart: your courage to act, to serve, and to heal. You are the hands and feet of Christ in the world. You remind us that love must look like something. Don't let yourself carry the world alone. The Savior role doesn't belong to you. Let others lift you. Let God replenish you.

Ask yourself:

- What motivates my acts of service — love or pressure?
- Where might I be rescuing others instead of partnering with them?
- How might Jesus be inviting me to receive love, not just give it?

If you're a **Unity Type**, we need your presence: your gift for peacemaking, for seeing the whole and holding people together. You create belonging and safety. You make communion visible. Don't lose your voice trying to keep everyone happy. Your perspective matters. Speak the truth and galvanize others in love.

Ask yourself:

- When have I chosen peacekeeping over true peace?
- What truth am I afraid to say?
- How might Jesus be inviting me to lead, not just support?

If you're a **Beauty Type**, we need your vision: your ability to find God in the unexpected, to draw others into reverence and awe. You help us pause, breathe, and see the sacred all around us. Don't forget to ground your wonder in truth. Beauty untethered can drift, becoming overly emotional, self-referential, or disconnected from reality. Truth gives beauty roots, not to confine it, but to steady and deepen its impact so your gift doesn't just inspire others, it transforms and unites the community around you.

Ask yourself:

- Where do I see God's beauty most clearly?
- Do I let truth challenge my preferences?
- How might Jesus be inviting me to speak with more clarity and courage?

When each of us lives from the Spirit and honors the gifts of others, the Church becomes radiant. It becomes a living icon of the Trinity: distinct, united, and overflowing with love.

So if you've ever felt like your way of loving was too much, too weird, too different—hear this:

You are needed.

Your gift matters.

The mission of the Church will only be complete when every person learns to receive and reflect the love of God in their own unique way.

Let's stop waiting for someone else to lead. Let's start becoming the people God made us to be—together.

The Church doesn't just need more volunteers, it needs more saints.

And the saint that the world needs next might just be you.

JONAH'S PARALLEL

A Mission Bigger Than Your Perfection

Jonah's life is messy. His call was rejected, his rescue dramatic, his obedience conflicted, and his acceptance of grace incomplete. Yet God used him. Nineveh repented. God's mercy prevailed, and Jonah was still a part of that story. Jonah's journey reminds us: you don't have to start perfect. You don't have to be sure. You just have to be willing to follow, to obey where you are, and to let God refine you over time. Your gift is not held back by your past — it is invited into God's ongoing story of redemption.

EPILOGUE

YOUR CALL TO LOVE

You've just walked a journey that began with curiosity — *Who am I?* — and ended with a clearer vision: *I am made in the image of Love Himself.*

You've discovered your unique way of seeing, receiving, and returning God's love. You've seen how Truth, Goodness, Unity, and Beauty are not abstract ideals, but the fingerprints of the Creator etched into your soul.

This journey isn't meant to stay on the page.

The next step is yours.

This is not just self-discovery – it's an invitation to a deeper encounter: with Christ, with yourself, and with others. And from that encounter, your mission begins.

I remember sitting in a small group a few years ago, feeling hesitant and vulnerable. We were sharing prayer requests, and when it was my turn, I said something like, "I know God is asking me to do something — it's pretty clear — but I don't want to do it. I'm scared. It feels unknown, and I can't see what's on the other side. I have no idea how any good could come from it."

After the group ended, a friend leaned over and quietly said, "I don't know what God is asking you to do, but I do know this: just go to Nineveh."

That one sentence pierced right through my resistance. It was simple, but it spoke directly to the fear and pride I hadn't yet named. It was the nudge I needed.

Not long after that, I began sharing my story of healing. I started writing. I began speaking. Doors opened that I never would've imagined — not because I forced them open, but because I finally said yes. In every yes, God showed up. Again and again.

You never know why God is calling you to something. You don't have to understand the outcome. You just have to trust the One who's calling. He always uses it for good.

> So wherever He's calling you — *whatever your Nineveh may be* — go.
> Go in love.
> Go in trust.
> Go knowing you are not alone.
>
> You are not too much or not enough.
> You are not just a number or a type.
> You are an image of God with a unique capacity to reveal His heart in the world.
>
> When each of us chooses to love as we were made, the Church is renewed.
> That's the call: not to be perfect, but to be present.
> To live in the Spirit.
> To love with your whole self.
>
> Because the world doesn't need more performance.
> It needs presence.

The more we each become who we were made to be, the more the Church becomes who She was made to be.

> So let this be the beginning — not the end.
> You are loved.
> You are chosen.
> You are needed.
> Now - go to Ninevah.

JONAH COMPANY

Transformation from the Inside Out

Jonah Company exists to help people and communities discover how they were made to love, and to live that call with courage and grace. Through the *Transcendental Types*™ framework and the *Spirit–Flesh Mindset*™ formation process, Jonah Company offers pathways for healing, renewal, and mission.

Our retreats, workshops, and leadership formation experiences are designed to help parishes, schools, ministries, and families build cultures of authentic love rooted in Catholic theology and the lived example of the saints.

NEXT STEPS

1. **Take the T-Types Assessment:** Explore how your unique spiritual lens shapes your relationship with God and others.
2. **Join a Retreat or Workshop:** Encounter Christ through teaching, prayer, and community.
3. **Invite Jonah Company:** We serve parishes, schools, and ministries with tailored events, leadership training, and family formation experiences.
4. **Stay Connected:** Learn more at transcendentaltypes.com and join the growing community of people saying "yes" to love.

ABOUT THE AUTHOR KRISTY MALIK

Kristy Malik is a Catholic speaker, writer, and co-founder of Jonah Company. A lifelong Catholic, she experienced a heart-level conversion in 2011 that reshaped her faith and mission. As far as Transcendental Types go, Kristy is an Orator (Truth 3), passionate about clarity, asking honest questions, and helping others live authentically in the love of God.

She is the co-creator of the *Transcendental Types framework* and corresponding tools that help people understand how they were made to love — and how to live it with freedom and purpose. Her work focuses on healing, identity, and spiritual formation, especially for women navigating faith and vocation in today's world.

Kristy has been featured on *Ascension Presents Daily Reflections*, the *Embrace Catholic Moms Conference*, and the Walking with Purpose YouTube series *Truth with Handles: The Conversation*, as well as events across the DC area and beyond.

At home, Kristy is a mom of five, navigating the beautiful chaos of family life with her college-sweetheart-turned-husband, Osama, — her favorite teammate in life and ministry.

APPENDIX

THE TWELVE TRANSCENDENTAL TYPES, DESCRIPTIONS, AND SAINTS

Truth 1 – The Commander

The Commander sees God as the ultimate source of truth and authority. They understand themselves as mission-driven leaders who seek loyalty and clarity. They view others through a lens of alignment with purpose, expecting shared commitment to the truth. Their time orientation is toward the future, always strategizing what must be done next. Motivated by the mind and strengthened by the will, they rely on prudence to act with purpose.

- **Gospel**: *"Everyone who listens to these words of mine and acts on them..."* (Matthew 7:24)
- **Saints**: St. Teresa of Calcutta, St. Charles Borromeo

Truth 2 – The Intellectual

The Intellectual experiences God as the fullness of wisdom and revelation. They see themselves as quiet stewards of knowledge, offering insight without needing recognition. They connect with others through thoughtful dialogue and truth, preferring depth to emotion. They are future-focused, contemplating long-term meaning and consequence. Their motivation arises from the mind, guided by prudence and a desire for coherence.

- **Gospel**: *"Do not think that I have come to abolish the law or the prophets..."* (Matthew 5:17)
- **Saints**: St. Thomas Aquinas, St. Scholastica

Truth 3 – The Orator

The Orator sees God as truth made beautiful, and delights in expressing that truth to others. They understand themselves as both thinkers and communicators who value relational engagement. They view others as fellow seekers of wonder, wanting to inspire and connect through story. They experience time in thoughtful reflection, balancing the past and future in how they teach. Their motivation is a blend of mind and soul, driven to make truth resonate.

- **Gospel**: *"He spoke to them at length in parables..."* (Matthew 13:3)
- **Saints**: St. Teresa Benedicta of the Cross (Edith Stein), St. Dominic

Beauty 1 – The Idealist

The Idealist sees God as perfect Beauty and longs to align with His justice and order. They see themselves as seekers of divine integrity, often struggling with the world's imperfections. Others are approached with a desire for mutual transformation and authenticity. Time is experienced with a longing for eternity, as they yearn for what could be. Motivated by the soul and guided by justice, they strive for wholeness in all things.

- **Gospel**: *"Whoever lives the truth comes to the light, so that his works may be clearly seen as done in God."* (John 3:21)
- **Saints**: St. Paul the Apostle, St. Rose of Lima

Beauty 2 – The Artist

The Artist encounters God in mystery and sacred awe, especially through sorrow and beauty. They understand themselves as vessels of sensitivity and creativity, shaped by memory. They relate to others through emotional resonance and compassion born of shared pain. Their time is past-oriented, often moved by nostalgia and longing. Motivated by the soul, they find purpose in expressing truth through beauty.

- **Gospel**: *"The Word became flesh and made his dwelling among us."* (John 1:14)
- **Saints**: St. Thérèse of Lisieux, St. John of the Cross

Beauty 3 – The Diplomat

The Diplomat sees God through the ideal of harmony and meaningful structure in relationships and society. They view themselves as bridges between people and ideas, longing to unify what is fragmented. They relate to others through thoughtful conversation and a vision of shared beauty. Time for them blends past reflection with a hope for future renewal. Motivated by the soul and mind, they are justice-seekers through relational wisdom.

- **Gospel**: *""I pray... that they may all be one, as you, Father, are in me and I in you... that they may be brought to perfection as one." (John 17:21–23)*
- **Saints:** Pope St. John Paul II, St. Elizabeth of Hungary

Unity 1 – The Enthusiast

The Enthusiast sees God as joyful communion and loves Him through delight in people. They understand themselves as bringers of joy and connection. Others are seen as companions in celebration and meaning. They are deeply present in the now, emotionally vibrant and relationally alive. Motivated by the heart, they radiate empathy and spirited encouragement.

- **Gospel**: *"At the moment the sound of your greeting reached my ears, the infant in my womb leaped for joy."* (Luke 1:44)
- **Saints**: St. Francis of Assisi, Servant of God Sister Clare Crockett

Unity 2 – The Peacemaker

The Peacemaker sees God as perfect unity and seeks Him through contemplation and peace. They view themselves as harmonizers who long for reconciliation in all things. Others are approached with gentleness and the hope of mutual understanding. They live with a timeless perspective, seeing the eternal thread in relationships. Motivated by the heart and soul, they create space for healing and communion.

- **Gospel**:*The Spirit of the Lord is upon me... He has sent me to bring glad tidings to the poor... to proclaim liberty to captives... to let the oppressed go free." (*Luke 4:18)
- **Saints**: St. Philip Neri, St. Catherine of Siena

Unity 3 – The Farmer

The Quiet Protector experiences God as steady, silent strength. They see themselves as background guardians who offer peace without needing to be seen. Others are held with tender loyalty and quiet endurance. They live between present and past, often reflecting deeply and letting time unfold slowly. Motivated by the heart and will, they bring courage in calm, hidden ways.

- **Gospel**: *"And Mary kept all these things, reflecting on them in her heart." (*Luke 2:19)
- **Saints**: St. Joseph, St. Kateri Tekakwitha

Goodness 1 – The Physician

The Physician experiences God as the great healer and source of all goodness. They see themselves as restorers, drawn to what is broken and compelled to fix it. They relate to others by identifying needs quickly and acting with courage. Their time focus is future-oriented, urgently moving toward healing and resolution. Motivated by the will and fortified by compassion, they thrive on taking immediate action.

- **Gospel**: *"Those who are well do not need a physician, but the sick do. I did not come to call the righteous but sinners."* (Mark 2:17)
- **Saints**: St. Theresa of Avila, St. Louis de Montfort

Goodness 2 – The Helper

The Helper knows God through quiet acts of kindness and the gentle presence of divine goodness. They understand themselves as nurturers who help good things grow. Others are seen with tender optimism, and they naturally support without needing attention. They live in the present, responding to needs as they arise with calm steadiness. Motivated by the will and heart, they act with grace and compassion.

- **Gospel**: *"No one is good but God alone."* (Mark 10:18)
- **Saints**: St. Elizabeth Ann Seton, St. Martin de Porres

Goodness 3 – The Defender

The Defender sees God as strong and just, a protector of what is right. They view themselves as guardians who quietly ensure safety and order. Others are approached with caution but loyalty, especially when entrusted to their care. Their time focus is toward the future, preparing for what might go wrong. Motivated by the will and a deep sense of courage, they act to preserve the good.

- **Gospel**: *"Truly this man was the Son of God."* (Mark 15:39)
- **Saints**: St. Joan of Arc, St. Ignatius of Loyola

Made in the USA
Coppell, TX
08 June 2026

78835140R00038